CW01302216

BOOK ANALYSIS

By Luke Hilton

Middlesex
by Jeffrey Eugenides

Bright Summaries.com

BOOK ANALYSIS

Shed new light
on your favorite books with

Bright
≡Summaries.com

www.brightsummaries.com

JEFFREY EUGENIDES	**9**
MIDDLESEX	**13**
SUMMARY	**17**

    From Bursa to Detroit
    The Zebra Room
    The Obscure Object
    Fluid Identity

CHARACTER STUDY	**25**

    Calliope/Callie/Cal
    Desdemona
    Lefty
    Milton
    Chapter Eleven

ANALYSIS	**35**

    Gender identity
    Fate
    America

FURTHER REFLECTION	**45**
FURTHER READING	**49**

JEFFREY EUGENIDES

AMERICAN NOVELIST

- **Born in Detroit, Michigan (USA) in 1960.**
- **Notable works:**
    - *The Virgin Suicides* (1993), novel
    - *The Marriage Plot* (2011), novel
    - *Fresh Complaint* (2017), short story collection

Jeffrey Eugenides is an American writer who began writing novels and short stories in the 1990s. His first novel, *The Virgin Suicides*, was published to critical acclaim and later became an internationally successful film directed by Sofia Coppola. The success of the novel and the film made Eugenides a household name and his next two novels received wide international readership, with *Middlesex* winning the prestigious Pulitzer Prize for Fiction in 2003. His work is notable for its attachment to his birthplace of Michigan. Many of his stories are set there and reflect the diverse nature of the state and, in particular, the city of Detroit. Many aspects of modern American culture originated in Detroit, such as Motown music and the automobile industry, and Eugenides references these in his work in order to build a colourful and rich background to the narrative.

MIDDLESEX

AN EXPLORATION OF FAMILY & IDENTITY

- **Genre:** novel
- **Reference edition:** Eugenides, J. (2003) *Middlesex*. London: Bloomsbury.
- **1st edition:** 2002
- **Themes:** gender, fate, modernisation, America, family

Eugenides' second novel is a family saga, depicting multiple generations of the Stephanides family as they move from the Old World amidst danger and war to a new and strange life in America. It builds many dichotomies into its structure, such as nature versus nurture, Old World versus New World, and male versus female, in order to ask questions about the basic understandings of contemporary life. The novel explores what life is like for intersex people, those who have both male and female biology, through the protagonist Cal (Calliope), who addresses the reader directly as he reveals the events in his family's lives that led to his condition.

The novel also questions fundamental understandings of American-ness by showing the attempted assimilation into a vastly different culture that presented itself to Cal's grandparents in 1922 when they moved to Detroit from a small town in Asia Minor. Eugenides gives the reader a richly detailed portrait of a family coming to terms with their own existence in a country and city that have troubles which are as complex as the troubles they themselves have. It is an interesting and, at over 500 pages, in-depth look at many different aspects of identity.

SUMMARY

FROM BURSA TO DETROIT

The novel begins with Cal telling the reader about his grandparents Lefty and Desdemona, and how, through many trials and tribulations, their actions led to his birth and his specific chromosomal abnormality. They are brother and sister and live high up over the city of Bursa in Asia Minor, surrounded by other Greeks. Desdemona weaves silk and Lefty goes out drinking and gambling, and avoiding the only two eligible women in the town. When a Turkish army comes through and things begin to get difficult, they decide to leave. On their way, they realise that they are in love with each other. At a port, waiting for passage to safety, the decide to be together. Nobody knows them on the boat, so they are able to pretend they have met and are courting. They are married on their way to New York City, where they have to prepare themselves for the immigration process.

Once they are safely in the country, they make their way to Detroit, where Sourmelina (their cousin) and her husband Jimmy Zizmo have agreed to take them in. Though Sourmelina is surprised that Lefty's mysterious bride she had heard about has turned out to be her own cousin and his sister, she agrees to keep their secret, not even telling her husband. Desdemona is sure that Sourmelina will keep their secret, as she has kept her secrets for her in the past. Though neither speaks English, they are quick to learn and Lefty especially becomes adept while working at the Ford plant in Detroit. Eventually he is laid off and goes into bootlegging alcohol with Jimmy. Desdemona and Sourmelina fall pregnant on the same night. When Sourmelina goes into labour Jimmy is not there, as he is arguing with Lefty, falsely accusing him of sleeping with his wife. They skid on some ice and Lefty escapes unharmed, but Jimmy's body disappears and they presume him dead.

THE ZEBRA ROOM

Desdemona and Lefty have two children together, but the relationship falters when she learns of an increased risk of birth defects in incestuous partnerships. Lefty opens a speakeasy called The

Zebra Room in their basement to cater for the drinkers during prohibition and spends more and more time there while his children grow up.

Years later, Desdemona and Lefty's son Milton is attempting to court Sourmelina's daughter Tessie, but she rejects him for a local Greek orthodox priest, Father Mike. Upset and looking to prove a point, Milton joins the United States Navy and goes to fight in World War 2. Tessie soon changes her mind and tells Desdemona that she loves Milton, and despite the fact that they are cousins Desdemona gives her approval. She only does so because she does not believe her son will return from the war. When he does return, they are married and Milton remains in the military. Tessie falls pregnant and they have their first child, a boy called Chapter Eleven (which is the only name we get for him). Desdemona is relieved when the boy is healthy and normal, as she gets anxious every time they have a child in the family. They then have their second child, a girl called Calliope. At first she appears to be a girl, and lives the first years of her life believing she is one. At the same time, Milton starts a restaurant to take over from Lefty's bar. Lefty feels useless because of the restaurant's initial success and develops a damaging gambling habit. The restaurant is in the middle of the area where the 1967 race riots of Detroit took place. It gets torched on a night during which the seven-year-old Calliope rides her bike there to check her father is okay.

THE OBSCURE OBJECT

As Calliope grows up and hits puberty, she begins to show more masculine signs than feminine ones, which is a source of great anxiety for her. Unsure as to what is happening to her body, she has two sexual experiences, one with a boy and the other with the boy's sister, who we are told Calliope refers to only as the Obscure Object. Calliope is fascinated by the desires she feels for the Obscure Object, and this adds to her confusion. When Calliope and the Obscure Object are caught in a compromising encounter, Calliope injures herself running away.

While treating her for the injury, the doctor discovers that Calliope is intersex and sends her to New York City for lots of invasive and embarrassing tests and assessments with specialists. The doctors believe that it is best that Calliope lives her life as a woman, since she has always been brought up as one. They schedule a gender-reassignment surgery to give Calliope a more convincing female anatomy, but she is afraid and runs away. She decides to live her life as a male and adopts the name Cal, instead of Calliope.

FLUID IDENTITY

At only 14, Cal hitchhikes across the country to San Francisco, where he gets involved in a burlesque show. Despite feeling and acting male, Cal's body is androgynous and compellingly beautiful, which makes him an ideal target for exploitation by the burlesque show's owner. People watch Cal swim around a tank like a mermaid, hoping to get a look at his unusual genitalia.

Eventually, the show is raided by the police, who arrest those involved, including Cal, for their part in the illegal sex work that was taking place there. When Cal is released, it is to his brother, Chapter Eleven. While Cal has been away, their father Milton was involved in a car accident and died. Cal reunites with his family and stands guard during the funeral, which is a task reserved for men, cementing Cal's identity as masculine.

Cal looks forward to his future life but proceeds with caution. Throughout the novel the reader is given snippets of Cal's life after the events of the novel have transpired. In these small portions of narrative Cal is dating a woman, and as they get serious he reveals the difficulties he experiences in becoming physical with female partners due to his unusual gender-biology. He explains that often things do not get to the point where he can become sexually active with women because of his anxieties about his body, an issue he attempts to cover up with stylish and masculine external affectations.

CHARACTER STUDY

There are lots of characters in *Middlesex* worthy of attention. Below are the five main characters who are central to driving the narrative forward.

CALLIOPE/CALLIE/CAL

As the central character of the novel, Cal is the intersex narrator who gives the primary meaning to the novel's title (the other being the family's home being called Middlesex). Cal is raised as a girl after being born a hermaphrodite, something he believes is a consequence of fate coupled with genetics, and reveals throughout the text the minutiae that lead to his conception and his gender realisation. After a normal childhood, his pre-pubescent stage is filled with anxiety over his appearance, which sometimes, because of his height and slender body, gives him "the posture of a fashion model" (p. 304) and at other times leaves him worried about "being left behind, left out" (p. 285). The failure in puberty to start a menstrual cycle fills both him and his parents with worry, to the point where he fakes a period in order to ease his mother's mind. A kind and bright child and teenager, brave enough to follow a tank into a riot at seven years old, he finds his appearance and gender identity too much to handle, hiding in the ornate bathroom stalls of his school, or behind his long un-cut hair. It is through Cal's early life that we see the difficulties of being born outside of societally accepted gender norms. Believing himself to be a girl until medical intervention reveals otherwise, Eugenides' depiction of Cal provides an insight into the life of a character with experiences far removed from the lives that most people live.

As a young adult, he parades his androgynous body to people in an illegal show. This experience is a contradictory account of the pleasure that one can cause others, as well as a degrading life, making a spectacle of himself and further alienating himself from societal norms. Although he eventually finds some semblance of peace, living life as a straight man and seeking relationships with women, the anxiety surrounding how he was born follows him to Berlin, a city that, like him, is both one thing and another. His continued gender anxiety manifests itself in repeated failure to consummate relationships due to his fear of the stigma attached to his situation. Despite this, through his narratorial voice, Eugenides shows that Cal finds some contentment in sharing his story and wondering about the other oppositions in his life that mirror his experience of gender.

DESDEMONA

Desdemona is Cal's paternal grandmother and one of the first non-narrator Stephanides family members that we meet. A proficient organiser of people's lives, she finds it difficult to cope with situations that she cannot manage. Her initial attempts at arranging a marriage for her brother Lefty are scuppered when the two of them reveal their sexual attraction towards one another, as well as by the impending military drama that overtakes their home of Bursa in Asia Minor. Her new life in America, her marriage to Lefty and the secret of her and Lefty's true relationship cause her immense guilt and shame, almost equal to the love she feels for him.

She is attached to the past in a way that no other character is. Her cousin and confidant Lina, who "[erased] just about everything identifiably

Greek about her[self]" (p. 84), represents the opposite to Desdemona, who represents the Old World of Europe and Greek mythology. It is her attachment to superstition that leads her to sour her marriage to Lefty in its early stages, believing that their union is immoral and will lead to negative consequences. Her refusal to comfortably be a wife to Lefty drives him into the illegal alcohol trade. This superstition, while accurate due to the circumstances of Cal's birth, is tested when Cal's mother Tessie falls pregnant. Desdemona's prediction of the gender of a child is never incorrect other than when she predicts that Cal will be a boy and yet he is born a girl. This failure seems to represent the death of the old-world magic for Desdemona, who is far less able to adapt than her husband. Desdemona's role in the novel is interesting: it is her prediction that is ultimately correct about Cal's gender, but her role in the genetic mutation is a fateful consequence of a marriage she felt guilty about to begin with. At times dramatic, her love for Lefty is truly revealed after his death, when she takes to her bed never to leave it, spending years wishing that she would die so that they could be together.

LEFTY

Lefty is Cal's paternal grandfather and a man he feels enormously close to while he is alive. His death coincides with the earliest portion of Cal's ongoing gender confusion, and thus seems to represent the death of his innocent ignorance. Lefty, however, is neither innocent nor ignorant. In Bursa he womanises, drinks and gambles, but all to compensate for his growing attraction to his sister. His happiness when she agrees to marry him is marred only by her unenthusiastic manner of conducting their marriage when they arrive in America. He is not married to the old-world ways of the Greeks in the same way that Desdemona is, and quickly adapts while working at the Ford factory, where he takes part in a performance celebrating various immigrants' successful transitions to Americanness. His language skills are well developed and he works on translations throughout his life, which he never lives to see through.

After losing his job at the Ford plant, he begins working with Lina's husband Jimmy Zizmo, a character whose criminality rubs off on Lefty. They begin rum-running during prohibition and he then opens a speakeasy. Unlike Jimmy, however, Lefty is neither a cruel nor a dangerous criminal, and he eventually lives out a dream of opening a small bar and diner in Detroit. After his son takes over the family business, he finds himself drawn back into the underworld, this time in the form of illegal gambling. He eventually loses all their money, so Desdemona and Lefty are forced to move in with their son and his family. This fall from grace is mirrored in his medical issues. After a stroke he loses the ability to speak, and has to write anything he wants to say onto a chalk board. Although this might seem like a loss of dignity, Lefty represents a calming presence in the Stephanides' otherwise chaotic lives. Cal regards his speechlessness as "an act of refinement", suggesting it "went with his elegant clothes" (p. 261).

MILTON

Milton is Cal's aggressive, politically right-wing father. He fights hard to gain the affection of his cousin Tessie, and proves his strength by joining the armed forces during World War 2. This militaristic outlook on life develops as he grows older and more conservative. A fan of Nixon and capitalism, he starts a hugely successful chain of hot-dog restaurants. It is through Milton that many of the novel's political and racial elements emerge. After the 1967 riots in Detroit, Milton begins to develop animosity towards the black residents of the city, accusing them of laziness and of being violent by nature. It is during these riots that we see his views on property and business. He barricades himself in his restaurant, which is at the epicentre of the violent riot, and tells a man who comes to see him that he is there because "I've gotta protect my property", to which the man replies "You life ain't you property?" (p. 245). This warped outlook on life and money leads Milton to be a stern father, disappointed and worried about his eldest child, Chapter Eleven, when he becomes involved in drugs and the anti-war movement.

Milton represents the last of the Greek identity dying out of his family. Although he names his hot-dog chain after the mythological figure of Hercules, he sides with America in an armed conflict involving the Greeks. This upsets the

Greek friends that he and Tessie have over for a traditional Greek meal every Sunday, and they never return. He renounces his Greekness in favour of his American identity, and follows this with a straight-edged approach to life and making money.

CHAPTER ELEVEN

Cal's older brother starts off life as a nerdy child who is smart, awkward and inexperienced (to the point that he asks to see his pre-pubescent sister's genitalia out of curiosity). As he grows up and goes to college, however, he develops a personality fuelled by anti-war sentiment and becomes a typical 'hippie' of the time. He tells Cal about his drug use and brings a girl home who is both vegetarian and openly critical of Milton's business practices. They accuse him of being an exploiter for only paying his employees minimum wage. This sparks an argument and the couple leave the family home.

Although Eugenides gives Chapter Eleven some fairly 'righteous' political perspectives, he seems less self-aware than his sister, basically ignoring the privilege that Milton's business has afforded him. In a similar way, compared with Cal's atypical life, Chapter Eleven seems to occupy fairly stereotypical roles for young men in America in the late 1960s/early 1970s. His drug use and politics ultimately make no difference to his family's wellbeing but he offers a counter-narrative, pointing at what Cal's life might have been like had he been born in a genetically typical body.

ANALYSIS

GENDER IDENTITY

Cal is the character through which we learn most about the struggles of gender identity. The novel often lets the political ramifications of being born intersex, or otherwise falling outside gender norms, take up less narrative space than the personal effects it has on Cal and his family. However, Cal as an adult male tells the reader that there is a political side to the issue that he finds it difficult to face:

> "Is it really my apolitical temperament that makes me keep my distance from the intersexual rights movement? Couldn't it also be fear? Of standing up. Of becoming one of *them*." (p. 319)

The intimacy that Cal derives from sharing his story with the reader could be seen as a direct response to the intimacy he does not feel he is able to get from society. This quote reveals the truth behind Cal's anti-political stance. He is afraid of the stigma that people like him have to face when they make themselves visible as being different from other people around them. The way in which he emphasises *them* makes it seem as though there is something less desirable and alien about these other people who share the same genetic traits as him. The fact that he does not believe he already is one of *them* implies a strong sense of disassociation within his sense of self-identity. By refusing to join with people in a struggle to make life better, he acknowledges his belief in society's inability to change, as well as a personal struggle to accept who he is. In his case, the personal and the political have interfered with one another. The significance of the adult Cal living in Berlin is reflected in the city's political divisions at the time of the novel's setting. Split into a communist and a Western city by the Berlin Wall, the overall picture of the city is distorted and difficult to find coherence in. Cal seems to see himself this way: born with traits of both sexes, he finds that he is unable to 'fit' with either one, and yet still refuses to fully side with the politics of the alternative intersex movement.

Middlesex also questions what the roles of each gender should be, and why society perceives them the way they currently do. The novel was written in 2002 but deals with themes that are still poignant today as the strength of the LGBT movement grows. Cal tells the reader that he has "the ability to communicate between the genders, to see not with the monovision of one sex but in the stereoscope of both" (p. 269), and this is a deliberate attempt on the part of Eugenides to make the reader question just what exactly each different gender would see. Although Cal views this as a sort of benefit of his condition, allowing him to know "what everyone was feeling" (*ibid.*), the reader is asked to wonder why a man would not empathise with a woman or vice versa. Cal is shown to exhibit stereotypical male attributes while being raised as a girl in the bravery shown in riding into a riot, and stereotypical female attributes in a high degree of pride in appearance as an adult male. In doing this, Eugenides' novel asks what about gender is acquired through birth, and what is acquired through the life one lives.

Mark Lawson writes "the cleverness of this DNA-trail is that moments which might otherwise be quaint or conventional – courtship, weddings, sex, [...] become subject to high tension" (Lawson, 2002). It is this tension which invites the reader to ask questions about gender, to challenge their preconceived notions. In making each situation that a young male or female goes through rich with dramatic tension, not only does Eugenides highlight the difficulties of living a life outside of the norm, but he also asks us as readers to question why the norm is what it is.

FATE

The idea of fate is bound up with Cal's sense of self-identity. The entire point of recounting his life story is to illustrate the hundreds of unlikely circumstances and situations that had to come to pass in order for his life to take shape in the way that it did. As well as a dedication to fate, Cal also seems to exhibit certain traits of an omniscient narrator, revealing future events to the reader before they have taken place, such as the first line of the novel: "I was born twice: first as a baby girl [...] then again, as a teenage boy"

(p. 3). This not only has the effect of ensuring that the reader will wish to continue reading, but also provides a further sense of awe and mystery behind Cal's existence.

Fate is suggestive of Cal's Greek heritage, and his and Desdemona's shared obsession with the course of history and the future implies a strong familial bond. However, Cal also uses fate and the changes over time to illustrate that other situations in his story share traits with his own biological condition. At one point, he states: "You used to be able to tell a person's nationality by the face. Immigration ended that" (p. 40). Here Cal suggests that the immigration of many people to the United States of America resulted in a blurring of nationalities, to the point where the face no longer contained clues to the person's identity. The obvious connection to be made here is that it was his grandparents' immigration that made his gender difficult to tell merely by looking at his face. Immigration in both senses seems to have affected identity, but not necessarily negatively or positively. While one could argue that the former situation is an obvious development of globalisation and the resultant immigration, and Cal's situation a highly atypical, personal event, Cal regards them as connected.

There are countless examples in *Middlesex* of Cal evoking fate to make suggestions about his own life, but one might well return to the idea of gender identity in order to explain it. For Cal, who has never been able to solve the riddle that he finds himself in, resting on fate and history to explain it becomes a way of developing a sense of identity wholly removed from the intersex movement he does not want to be part of. It is both a grandiose sense of self, and a way of coping with the feeling that he does not fit in.

AMERICA

The novel has two obvious ways of setting America in opposition to Greece, both in terms of different ways of life and different beliefs. The first is through Cal's grandparents, who make the move in order to flee the violence of the Old World for the belief in the safety of the new. The American Dream that Desdemona and Lefty have is exemplified in their words when they decide to make the journey: "Maybe here people won't be killing each other every single day" (p. 76). The irony is obvious, given inner-city America's reputation for violence, especially during periods of heightened racial tension. Despite this, the hope shared by the new incestuous couple is genuine, and they believe their new life will be full of happiness. Although there are certainly positives experienced by the couple, their lives are not as simple as the American Dream suggested they might be. Eugenides makes the direct comparison between the Old World and the new, which seems to favour the Greek method of doing things: "Historical fact: people stopped being human in 1913. That was the year Henry Ford put his cars on rollers" (p. 95). The automisation of work experienced in Detroit is in stark contrast to the work the couple did in Greece, where Desdemona's expertise in silk production was valued and she worked from start to finish on a product. The reality of the life first experienced in America for Lefty, however, is one in which the work done makes one fee less human.

The second way in which American experience is contrasted with that of Greek life is through Milton, especially his time spent before, during and just after the race riots. Before he renounces his Greek identity, Milton already displays certain attitudes of the white middle classes. He instructs Lefty not to let Cal come to see him at the diner any longer, because he chooses not to trust the black man with whom she spends time talking. The events of the riot are used by Milton as a "shield" against any different opinions to his own, "applicable not only to African Americans, but to feminists and homosexuals" (p. 246). Rather than learn about the other group with whom he has a problem, he uses his perceived notions as facts to attack them. This 'us versus them' attitude is reminiscent of the attitudes of the Greeks to the Turks that is explored in the first few chapters. The racial tension seems to follow the family from the Old World to the new, suggesting more similarities than Milton might care to acknowledge. A final contrast relating to the riots comes from the television; we are told that, amid burning buildings and death, "the mood wasn't one of desperation. I'd never seen people so happy in my entire life" (p. 240). The reference to the burning and murder that took place in Asia Minor is juxtaposed with the American looting that came with the race riots.

Although he would not condone the stealing, it follows a similar logic of consumerism to Milton's beloved capitalism.

Ultimately, *Middlesex* illustrates that, just like Cal, America is not only one thing. It is a place of opportunity, but also a place of repression, violence and hatred. It is a place where love can blossom, but also one where tensions develop. Just as Cal is at the same time male and female, so too is America. America is black and white and rich and poor. The Stephanides are American but they are also Greek. Eugenides' repeated use of oppositions reinforces this idea that people are not just one thing or another but a rich mixture of many different experiences. Laura Miller describes this as the novel's "utopian reach" (Miller, 2002) and argues that it is the novel's insistence on not seeing things in black and white that makes it "deliriously American" (*ibid.*).

FURTHER REFLECTION

SOME QUESTIONS TO THINK ABOUT...

- Do you think that Lefty and Desdemona acted wrongly in having their children? Why/why not?
- What do you think Cal's life would have been like had he not been born intersex?
- What are some of the main oppositions presented to the reader in *Middlesex*?
- How does the novel explore racial identity?
- What are your impressions of the city of Detroit from reading the novel?
- What Greek mythology is present in the novel, and what do you think the significance of it is?
- Do you think Eugenides offers a fair representation of life for intersex people, despite not being intersex himself? Why/why not?
- Can you think of any other novels that deal with themes of intersexuality or incest? How do they compare to *Middlesex*?
- Do you think there is a thematic connection between the modernisation of America over the course of the novel, and Cal's condition? Explain your answer.

*We want to hear from you!
Leave a comment on your online library
and share your favourite books on social media!*

FURTHER READING

REFERENCE EDITION

- Eugenides, J. (2003) *Middlesex*. London: Bloomsbury.

REFERENCE STUDIES

- Lawson, M. (2002) Gender Blender. *The Guardian.* [Online]. [Accessed 1 February 2019]. Available from: <https://www.theguardian.com/books/2002/oct/05/featuresreviews.guardianreview15>
- Miller, L. (2002) My Big Fat Greek Gender Identity Crisis. *The New York Times.* [Online]. [Accessed 1 February 2019]. Available from: <https://www.nytimes.com/2002/09/15/books/my-big-fat-greek-gender-identity-crisis.html>

Although the editor makes every effort to verify the accuracy of the information published, BrightSummaries.com accepts no responsibility for the content of this book.

© BrightSummaries.com, 2019. All rights reserved.

www.brightsummaries.com

Ebook EAN: 9782808017909

Paperback EAN: 9782808017916

Legal Deposit: D/2019/12603/62

Cover: © Primento

Digital conception by Primento, the digital partner of publishers.

Printed in Great Britain
by Amazon